D0521732

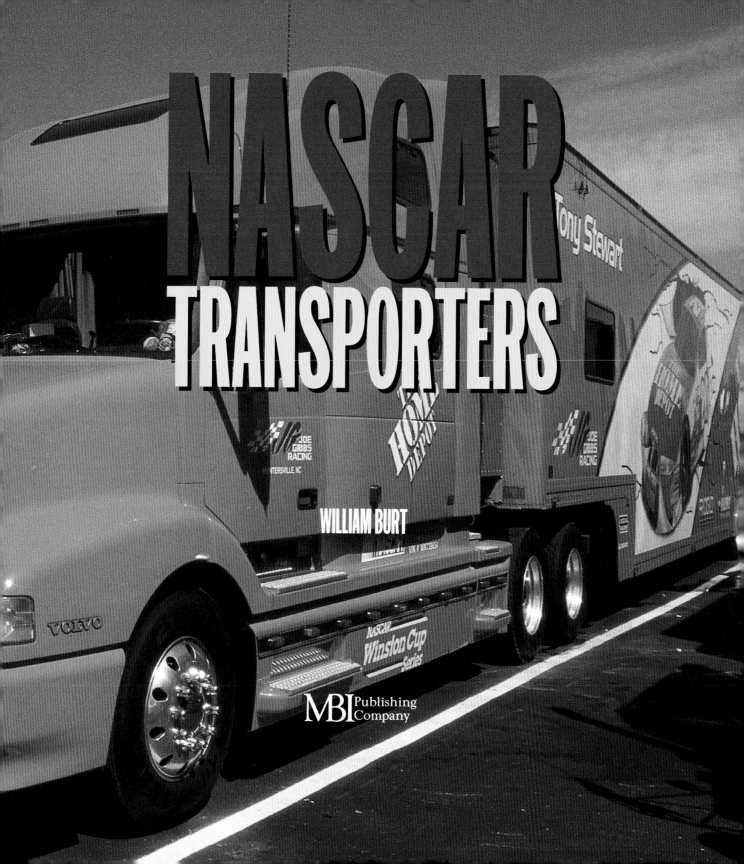

NASCAR
TRANSPORTERS

WILLIAM BURT

MBI Publishing Company

First published in 2000 by MBI Publishing Company, 729 Prospect Avenue, PO Box 1, Osceola, WI 54020-0001 USA

MBI Publishing Company books are also available at discounts in bulk quantity for industrial or sales-promotional use. For details write to Special Sales Manager at Motorbooks International Wholesalers & Distributors, 729 Prospect Avenue, PO Box 1, Osceola, WI 54020-0001 USA.

Library of Congress Cataloging-in-Publication Data Available

ISBN 0-7603-0816-0

On the front cover: The first piece of equipment of any race team to arrive at the track and the last one to leave is the team's transporter. Next to the car, the transporter is the team's most crucial piece of hardware. Not only must it move the racecars and equipment; it must also carry everything in a very organized manner for quick access. If a particular piece of hardware doesn't make it on the trailer, the entire race might be lost due to poor planning.

On the frontispiece: Until the team's 80,000-pound load arrives safely at the track, the fate of any superstar driver is in the hands of his or her transporter's driver. When the rig fires up to begin the over-land haul, there has to be a moment in the heart of every crew chief for a prayer to insure the load's safe arrival.

On the title page: In the early days of stock car racing, you ran what you drove to the track. This is not the case today. Almost every brand of semi on the market is used to haul cars, equipment, and personnel to the track. It's not just American tractors doing all the hard work in this American sport—Joe Gibbs Racing uses the latest and best offerings from the Swedish manufacturer Volvo.

On the back cover: You can only bring so much to the track so a transporter *has* to be multi-functional. The top of the trailer does more than keep the rain out of a Winston Cup transporter. The rear of most trailers have been built tough to allow it to be used as a viewing platform. Crew chiefs and family members enjoy a bird's eye view as their driver attempts to turn the fastest lap times.

Edited by John Adams-Graf
Designed by Tom Heffron
Layout by Rebecca Allen

Printed in China

CONTENTS

INTRODUCTION

First In . . . Last Out

There are many things to admire in NASCAR's Winston Cup Division. It's no wonder that the race cars and drivers get most of the attention. The cars and engines are hand-built by many different teams, yet having the entire starting lineup qualify for a race within a half-second of each other is common. The drivers, while always racing at the limit of the equipment, also drive with a surgical precision,

Left and above
Some things in the stock car racing world have changed and others haven't. The equipment necessary to compete in today's top venues is light-years beyond what was necessary in the 1950s; results, however, are often the same. *Talladega Motorsports Hall of Fame*

A cross between a factory and a laboratory, the modern Winston Cup team's shop affords engineers and mechanics just about every available tool and material. Teams now have everything from computerized machining and diagnostic equipment to time in a wind tunnel. The result is that the next mile per hour of speed that can be tweaked out of the car will be more expensive than the previous one.

running incredibly consistent lap times while speeding just inches apart on a crowded race track.

In recent years the crew chiefs, team members, and pit crews have begun to receive more and more well-deserved recognition for the huge contribution that they make to a winning effort. As the sport has grown, equipment that the teams use has also become an area of interest. First, the media highlighted the pit equipment during technical segments of race broadcasts. It is now very common for racing news programs to tape shows on location at a team's shop. Indeed, many fans vacation in the Charlotte, Concord, and Mooresville areas primarily to take advantage of shop tours when they are available. However, anyone who has done this for a few years does not have to be told that times have changed. Over the last 30 years the equipment the teams use

has evolved dramatically. It has become more precise, more thorough, and a heck of a lot more expensive.

However, as far as equipment goes, the transporter may be the biggest workhorse on a Winston Cup equipment list, while receiving very little attention. Transporters, too, have changed dramatically over the last few years and have become an integral part of fielding a Winston Cup team.

The transporter is the first piece of equipment to arrive at the track and the last one to leave. Not only must it move the race cars and equipment, it must also carry the equipment in a very organized manner for quick access. Time at the track is limited and therefore very valuable. It cannot be wasted

To get the race cars, tools, and gear to the track, the Winston Cup teams rely on long-haul tractors and 53-foot transporters. With the exception of the paint jobs, the tractors are like their commercial counterparts, but the transporters are built specifically for Winston Cup applications.

Pack in around 45 Busch Series tractors and transporters and 45 Winston Cup Series tractors and transporters. Unload the race cars, tools and gear, all of the track personnel, NASCAR officials, and a Goodyear store, then stir in a couple thousand people, and you have a short-track garage area. The place is crowded and workspace is limited, but teams cannot let it affect their performance. Championship points here count just as much as those earned in the Daytona 500.

looking for equipment or having to go buy or borrow a part or tool. Transporters must be efficiently designed so that every bit of space is used. As racing has become more competitive, it has become more complex. This means more and more parts and tools are required.

In many teams, getting everything to the track in its proper place is the responsibility of the truck driver, but it takes a solid team effort to carry it off. Obviously, transporting the load *safely* to the track on time is important, but a transporter performs another function that may be just as critical: it is a home away from home for the crew members.

One of the less glamorous aspects of Winston Cup racing is the grueling travel schedule and the long work hours. The days start early on the road. Race weekends are usually three days long, and each day the garage opens at 6 A.M. The team members are always lined up to get in. This usually means getting up between 4 and 5 A.M., depending on how close the hotel is to the track. The day often will not end until late in the evening. There are currently 34 races in a Winston Cup season, plus the Bud Shootout, the Gatorade 125 qualifying races at Daytona, and the Winston. To compete in all of these events, the teams will spend about 113 days during the 9 1/2-month-long season at the track, which does not include testing or travel days. During this time the only constant is the transporter. It truly becomes the closest thing to a home that the team has.

The transporter is the center of activity throughout the race weekend. It is where crews discuss the setups and eat lunch. It is a viewing platform for the teams during practice and qualifying. It is a meeting place, a workshop, a kitchen, and sometimes most important of all, it is a place to get away from the crowds and the hustle and bustle of life in the garage. One of the keys to concentration and teamwork is the elimination of distractions. Anyone who has spent time in Winston Cup garage areas knows that they are full of distractions. There is the normal commotion associated with qualifying and practicing 45 to 50 race cars. On top of that, there are clamoring fans, press, and vendors and all other sorts of support personnel. It can be very important for crew members to have somewhere to escape to for a few minutes. It is this simple function that may make the transporter one of the most important pieces of equipment that a team owns. At every race the transporter is the first place crew members go to when they arrive at the track and the last place they visit before they leave.

Sometimes the transporter is just a place to relax. Racing teams spend a great deal of time on the road, and the transporter becomes more than a trailer; it becomes their home. The transporter can be the only consistent item in Winston Cup's ever-changing surroundings.

CHAPTER 1

THE EVOLUTION OF THE TRANSPORTERS

Form Follows Function . . .

Drivers and mechanics have not always had the luxuries that are afforded to them today. Perhaps there is more pressure and higher stakes than ever in NASCAR racing, but the parts and tools with which the team must accomplish the job have improved. Better parts and tools for the team means higher speed and better handling for the driver. It also means more consistency throughout the field. The gap between the fastest car and the slowest gets smaller. As a result, the competition becomes even fiercer, and when the competition is this tight, *if you are standing still you are going backwards!*

This intense competition, combined with the continued popularity of the sport, has led to many changes in Winston Cup racing over the past 40 years, and there is no equipment that has changed more than the transporter. It became not as much a luxury as a necessity. Changes in transporter technology not only reflect a

Driving and maintenance were more of a chore with the earliest transporters. This four-horsepower model took the Number 15 car over some tough roads getting to the track. Since men began racing cars, they have been looking for the perfect vehicle to get them to the track. The result has been a steady precession of improvements in carrying capacity and ergonomics. *Talladega Motorsports Hall of Fame*

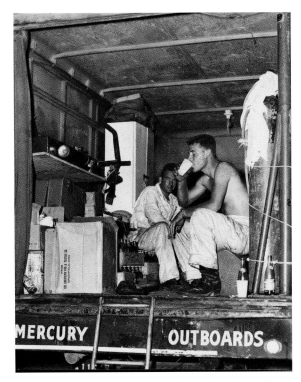

The accommodations have not always been as luxurious as they are today. A borrowed truck usually offered no frills, but it got the team and equipment to the track and gave members a place to collect their thoughts. *Talladega Motorsports Hall of Fame*

As much as a place to work, a hauler is a place for the team to relax during the few slow times at the track. Before there were transporters, team members had to find any spot that they could to relax. *Talladega Motorsports Hall of Fame*

different way to carry the car and equipment to the track; they also reflect how the sport itself has changed.

Many of the early NASCAR racers often drove their cars to the track with a few spare parts in the back seats. (Some might even drive these same cars to work on Monday, if the vehicles were still in one piece). As the cars developed more and more into pure racing machines, they were hauled to the track on any type of trailer that would fit the bill. This usually meant a flatbed truck or trailer, bought or borrowed for weekend use. Some of the wealthier racers began to modify and customize their trailers. Early modifications ranged from built-in tool cabinets and tire racks to fancy paint jobs. For many years the starting lineups of most races were filled with what would now be considered amateur teams. Most of the cars had few or no sponsors and were put together, usually by the driver, for no reason other than enjoyment.

As the popularity of the sport grew, so did the desire for companies to sponsor racing teams. This further fueled the competition. The team's finishing position determined more than bragging rights; it began to determine the team's income. So, as racing moved from hobby to career, winning races became more and more important. As a result, more and more resources were invested in equipment.

Perhaps the biggest single event that cast the die for the evolution of the transporters was when NASCAR changed to the modern points system. NASCAR's premier series has not always been organized as it is today. In the early years there were often more than 50 races a year. It was not until the modern points systems that drivers were truly rewarded for attending and finishing every race. As a result, it was not necessarily a complete disaster if the car ran poorly at a particular event. Drivers did then what many prudent amateur dirt track racers still do: They park the car before it gets torn up, take it home and work on it, and have it in one piece the next week. Then maybe it will run better. However, beginning in 1972 the championship was based on how the drivers finished in all of the events. They were rewarded points for finishing positions and number of laps run. This completely changed the teams' strategies. Every position on the track meant more points at the end of the year, so each team fought hard for each position. Even the car running dead last still had a reason to race.

Prior to the championship point system, crews were not concerned about having enough parts to fix a car after a wreck in order to get back on the track and finish 35th instead of 40th. Now, crews work at breakneck speed to get a crashed car back in the race—not to win, but to salvage as many championship points as possible. Those points can mean the difference between winning the championship and finishing as runner-up. Just ask Bill Elliot, who lost the 1992 championship to Alan Kulwicki. Their points battle was not decided until the last race, and Kulwicki's margin of victory was only 10 points.

As Winston Cup racing continued its competitive growth, cars became better and better. More teams began to come to the track with very good equipment. The difference between good performance and poor performance in an environment as competitive as Winston Cup racing can often be measured in how many of the little things a team does right. Crews spent more and more time refining the race cars, which meant more parts were needed. If Team A has 10 sets of springs and Team B has 5, then Team A will likely have an advantage, because it will have more possible setups and thus can tune its car better. Transporters could get those valuable parts to the track.

Another force in the evolution of transporters was corporate sponsorship of racing teams. Ultimately, the addition of sponsorship only fueled the competitive fires both on and off of the track. The "43" car was still Richard Petty's racer, but it also became the "STP Pontiac." Image became a factor, because not only did the team speak for itself, it spoke for the sponsor as well. As much as any element of NASCAR racing, the haulers show the impact of corporate America on the sport. A $20,000 paint job does not make the race car go faster, but it does solidify the image of the team with the sponsor's product, and it makes the sponsor's product look good. Racing is just like the space program: speed costs money (*If there's no bucks ($), there's no Buck Rogers*), and

Over the years, many types of vehicles have been used to get race cars to the track. With STP as a sponsor, Richard Petty's team experimented with a few different types.

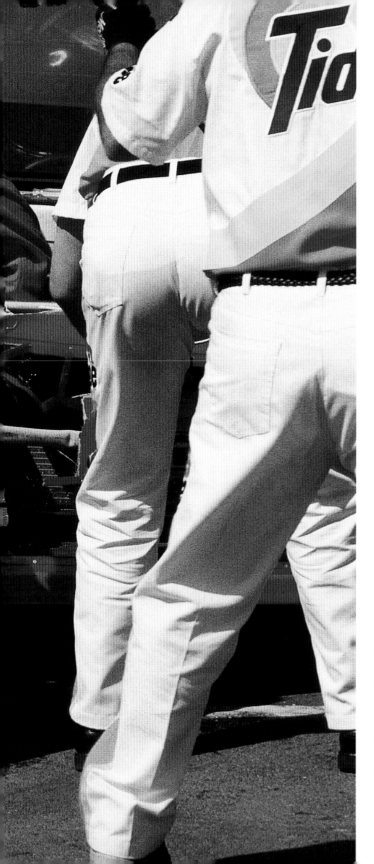

the money comes from the sponsors. While it is the goal of the team to win races, it is the goal of the sponsor to link its image with the excitement, competition, and fun of Winston Cup racing.

Who knows how many people see the rigs on the way to the race? I have been fortunate enough to spend a good bit of time around racing, yet I still find myself gawking when the new ones come out every year. Sponsoring a race team is like any other advertising that a company does. There must be a return on the investment. It is difficult to say what the ultimate impact is on a 12-year-old Bobby Labonte fan when he sees that big green and black transporter with flames all over it come barreling down the interstate. I think in its own small way it does increase the odds that that young fan eventually will drive a Pontiac and that when the OEM battery goes dead, he will probably replace it with an Interstate Battery. Sponsorship is funny. I use Tide detergent, even though that brand no longer sponsors Ricky Rudd. There are other good detergents on the market, but Tide supports racing. For some reason that makes a difference. Backing a racing team is also a visible expression of pride for a company. It has much more personality than six or eight Super Bowl commercials, which would roughly cost the same as sponsoring a NASCAR team for a year. Because of the tangible nature of this advertising, companies want it done right. Chances are that at some point in the season the transporter with "Budweiser" on the side will be parked next to the one with "Miller" on its side. It is a safe bet that the CEOs from either company do not want to be outdone by the other.

This brings us to the final factor that has influenced the evolution of the transporters: showmanship. The truth of the matter is that the people who own race teams are very successful in other businesses. They are usually men

The modern championship points system requires that a crew try frantically to get a wrecked car back onto the track. This means having the parts and equipment to deal with any eventuality at the track.

Following pages
By the 1990s, the transporters had reached a new level. They offered everything: capacity, flexibility, comfort—and they did it all while doubling as 53-foot, 70-mile-per-hour billboards.

with deep, vast resources who like to surround themselves with the latest technology. Translated, this means that they are kids at heart, are filthy rich, and love shiny new toys. In other words, they are a transporter salesman's dream.

As a result of such showmanship, the status of a team became somewhat judged by the type of equipment that it had. A fancy transporter certainly helped this image. I stress the word "status" and do not mean to confuse it with "success." There are a lot of teams out there with every resource available, yet they don't win races. As with most things in life, success is more a result of the effort that the people put in than a tally of the money spent on equipment. If expensive features on a snazzy trailer help the team work more efficiently and communicate better at the track, they can be counted as a factor toward success. Otherwise, the trailer is nothing more than a shiny new toy.

Whatever the cause, transporters have evolved from flatbed trailers to 53-foot-long shops on wheels. This steady wave of improvement has meant on-board compressors, generators, satellite dishes, refrigeration, microwaves, complete climate control, and very comfortable lounges. All of these features were added while still leaving enough room to carry all of the gear. Oh, yeah—there is still a small place at the top of the transporter to carry the race car.

Above and right
As the sport became more complex, there was a greater need for cargo capacity. Note the difference between the pit stops of yesteryear and today. *Talladega Motorsports Hall of Fame*

CHAPTER 2

LONG-HAUL TRACTORS

Pulling Their Weight . . .

Winston Cup teams use long-haul tractors that, aside from their paint jobs, are usually identical to their less radically decorated commercial counterparts. However, while the tractors are standard off-the-shelf equipment, the top teams tend to have the top-of-the-line-with-every-available-option standard off-the-shelf equipment.

A tour through a Winston Cup garage shows that the tractors used by the top teams reflect the cutting edge of modern long-haul tractor technology. They also represent some of the best and most outlandish paint jobs ever seen on commercial trucks.

All of the trucks used by the Winston Cup teams have a few things in common. They all have 10 wheels (2 front wheels and 8 drive wheels) and all are diesel powered. Practically all of the major manufacturers of long-haul tractors can be seen in the garage area of a Winston Cup event. Ford, Freightliner, Kenworth, Mack, Peterbilt, and Volvo have all been represented. The type of race car the team runs may determine the type of tractor that will pull the transporter to the race. Often a Ford tractor

An intimidating sight coming out of the night. The tractor, trailer, and cargo all add up to a total of 80,000 pounds.

Every year the tractors meet at 34 racing events on the regular NASCAR Winston Cup schedule. They will also occasionally gather at testing dates, both at the track and wind tunnel.

will pull a Ford team's transporter. However, chances are a Ford tractor will never be seen pulling the transporter of the Number 3 car, sponsored by GM Goodwrench.

In any hauling application, whether purely commercial or pulling a race car to the track for the weekend, the primary requirements of a tractor have always been to have enough power to handle the load safely and to be dependable. In either application, a breakdown will cost money and time. For a Winston Cup team, a breakdown will obviously mean the expense of the repair and the extra expense of renting another tractor to pull the transporter. But more importantly it could cost a team valuable time at the track, which is unthinkable. As a result, the tractors used by the Winston Cup teams tend to be newer models with all of the options. This means lower miles on the chassis and fewer hours on the engine. Winston Cup teams' tractors are also well maintained. Just like the family car, these truck require oil changes, filter changes, proper lubrication, and other periodic maintenance. For the teams with the greater financial resources, frequent tractor (and transporter) upgrades are common. Their trade-ins, which are often in near-perfect condition, are usually bought by other Winston Cup or Busch Grand National teams, repainted, and put back into service.

While there are differences between tractors of different makes, most are quite similar. They are usually quite agile, with sharp turning radiuses. On some trucks the front wheels can turn up to 45 degrees for superb close-quarter maneuvering. All eight of the rear wheels are drive wheels. The driveshaft supplies power to two differentials, one on each axle. The frames of the tractors are built of heavy steel with thicknesses ranging from 5/16 inch up to 5/8 inch in high-stress areas. The cab and the sleeper are built as separate units and mounted onto the frame. By using modern lightweight materials, a long-haul tractor with a sleeper can weigh less than 15,000 pounds. A tractor will probably have a maximum front axle load of around 12,000 pounds and a maximum rear axle load of around 34,000 pounds.

The long-haul tractor world is just like the racing world in one respect: More and more attention is being paid to aerodynamics. The better the body tractor cuts through the wind, the better fuel mileage the tractor gets. Over the operating life of a long-haul tractor, an increase of just one mile per gallon may be measured in the thousands of dollars.

Engine size and configuration vary between manufacturers. Most are inline six-cylinders that are both fuel-injected and turbocharged. Horsepower and torque numbers vary, depending on manufacturer and engine models. A couple of examples of engines currently on the market are the 14.9-liter Mack E7-460 Econodyne engine, rated at 460 horsepower at 1,600–1,800 rpm and producing 1,660 ft-lb of torque at 1,200 rpm; and the Kenworth T-2000's power plant, a 12.7-liter six-cylinder, which produces 500 horsepower at 2,100 rpm and 1,650 ft-lb of torque at 1,200 rpm. The engine alone in most tractors will weigh more than 2,000 pounds dry.

A huge radiator, usually more than 1,200 square inches, keeps the engine coolant temperature low. As a result of tractor manufacturers' efforts to cut weight, many trucks now have aluminum radiators. By replacing the steel radiator they may recognize a 50- to 60-pound weight savings.

Power transmission is usually through a clutch and manual transmission. On the Kenworth T-2000, power is transmitted from the engine to the wheels through a 10-speed gearbox and a 15-inch, 7-spring ceramic

Almost every brand on the market is represented at the track. Not just American tractors are represented in this American sport; Joe Gibb's Racing uses the latest and best offerings from Volvo.

A quick glance at the tag lets you know whose car is in this rig. Personal touches can be seen all over the tractors and transporters, even though it is pulling for a specific team.

clutch. The driveshaft runs to two 3.70-to-1 gears.

To slow the tractors down, they have large-drum air brakes front and rear, and many now have antilock systems. Air for the pneumatic systems is supplied by a compressor, which is mounted to and powered by the tractor's main engine.

A common tire size is the 11R24.5. This tire is 11 inches wide, is mounted on a 24.5-inch rim and has a diameter of 41.3 inches.

Today's long-haul tractors require less servicing than their ancestors did. With modern electronic engine controls, tune-ups are rare. Even when something goes wrong, truck designers strive to make fixing the problem

Opposite
Nothing matches a Peterbilt's classic look, with lots of chrome and lights. What it gives up in aerodynamics, it certainly makes up in classic, good looks.

Following pages
A statement from Penske Racing and Miller Lite. On a sunny day this transporter can blind you. The Freightliner tractor is fully skirted, with the drive wheels almost completely covered on the outside. Unlike many transporters, the sides are completely void of smaller stickers. The only companies represented on the tractor are Penske Racing and Miller Lite, the primary sponsors.

There is nothing "light-duty" about the frame of a long-haul tractor. It takes a great deal of strength to support the load, let alone to do it for years and suffer no damage.

The tractor's hood pivots forward for easy access. This gives mechanics a great deal of space in which to work.

The right side of the engine. The air compressor, which supplies the tractor's and transporter's pneumatic systems, is driven with engine power.

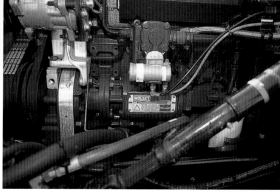

The left side of the diesel engine. Note the large air cleaner housing on the upper left firewall. The girth of the air compressor iis evident in the inset on the right.

as simple as possible. Kenworth advertises that in its T-2000 tractor, the blower motor, heater core, and evaporator core can be removed in seven minutes, without having to disconnect the air conditioning lines. This eliminates the time and expense of having to recharge the system.

The interiors of modern trucks are incredible. The comfort afforded truck drivers today is gracious compared to what was available 20 or 30 years ago. Modern tractors have two main areas, the cab and the sleeper. Cab construction varies between different manufacturers. Some manufacturers still believe in the strength of steel, galvanized for long life. Other companies, to lower the weight of the cab, now construct them from aluminum, either welded, riveted, or both. Every pound shaved from the tractor translates into more cargo that can be carried in the transporter, and aluminum does have the advantage of

being both lighter than steel and rust-free. Most brands of tractors, both steel and aluminum, sport a fiberglass hood, another rust-free, weight-saving measure.

The windshields of modern tractors have gotten larger, allowing for better visibility. The modern conventional trucks have hoods that are much more dramatically sloped than their predecessors. This not only provides better aerodynamics but also offers the driver the visibility of a cab-over design and the better ride and safety of a conventional truck.

The cabs are roomy. Inside dimensions for trucks can be 6 1/2 feet wide in the cab and 7 feet wide in the sleeper. This roominess allows some elbow room for even the biggest of drivers. Most cabs are designed with a passageway, around 30 inches wide, between the seats. This "hall-way" opens into the sleeper, allowing quick access for both driver and passenger.

Because the driver will spend most of his time driving, the seat is where the comfort starts. Most trucks come from the factory equipped with air cushion seats. These seats are mounted on air shocks to cushion the driver by dramatically dampening vibration, which in turn reduces driver fatigue. Because drivers spend so much time in one place, tractor manufacturers try to make the seat and its surrounding area as comfortable and user-friendly as possible. Seats usually feature adjustable armrests, kidney support, lumbar support, and thigh extensions, and are often heated as well. Most trucks now also feature both tilt and telescoping steering wheel for further driver comfort.

With all of the gauges and controls, the cabs of today's tractors often look more like an airplane cockpit than a truck interior. Many trucks now feature wraparound dashes designed to allow for quick and easy viewing. This means big well-lit gauges and controls set where the driver can easily see them.

All trucks have the same standard gauges that we find in cars, including speedometer, tachometer, fuel level, water temperature, oil pressure, and voltmeter (and/or an ammeter). However, long-haul trucks may also include gauges that display air cleaner and air supply status, exhaust temperature, oil temperature (for engine, transmission, and axles), fuel filter status, and manifold pressure. Of course the driver usually has a top-of-the-line AM/FM/WB radio and a powerful CB radio.

The second part of the tractor interior is the sleeper. In years past the sleeper was usually just a bunk, crammed in behind the cab as an afterthought to give the driver somewhere to sleep without having to rely on a hotel room. Truck manufacturers have now developed the living quarters of the tractor to the point that the driver's station now appears to be an afterthought. Cabs are open to the sleeper compartment through what amounts to a hallway between the driver and passenger seats. This passageway takes the driver or passenger into the sleeper, which often features standing headroom. Some, like the Kenworth T-2000, have a bed that is 7 feet long, 42 inches wide and sports a real spring mattress. Some sleepers are also outfitted with an additional fold-down upper bunk so that two people can catch some shuteye at the same time. By using a web belt restraint in the front of the bed, one driver can sleep while the other keeps the truck moving down the road.

The sleeper is not only a good place to sleep: it is also a fine place to relax. With a television, a VCR, and a refrigerator, all surrounded by plush diamond pattern upholstery and wood trimmed cabinets, the sleeper is a nice refuge on the road. The driver can "button up" the cab with curtains drawn or can keep the many windows open to afford the best view. Both the sleeper and cab are very well insulated to keep temperatures consistent and road noise to a minimum. Storage cabinets, bins, and closets are located wherever space allows and give the driver ample area to store essential gear. While at the track the sleeper is one of the few hiding places that the driver and crew can take advantage of. Any area that a person can escape to for a few minutes of peace and quiet is greatly appreciated. When traveling to tracks that are relatively close to the team's shop, the sleeper will most likely be filled with gear.

Opposite
Sleepers may also be accessible through a back door as well as through the cab.

CHAPTER 3

THE TRANSPORTER

Shelter from the Storm . . .

If a team is going to compete on the Winston Cup circuit, it must have a transporter. At the track, the team members will face many obstacles, and it is from the contents of the transporter that they must find solutions.

Teams who order their transporters from companies such as Featherlite Trailers can have them custom built, configuring the interior of the transporter the way they want it. Other teams get by just fine buying perfectly good used trailers from the top teams, who buy new transporters every couple of years. When purchased new, the trailer arrives with the cabinets, drawers, and most of the electrical system completely fitted. However, there is a great deal of customizing work to be done before the team can head to the track. Usually the first order of business is to paint both the transporter and the tractor.

Throughout any race weekend, the transporters will be the center of activity. During the Winston Cup schedule, over 9 months or about 35 weeks, the transporter is the only constant, and it becomes the team's home. Here the crew of the 99 car celebrates a birthday while competing at Talladega.

The practical advertising and first-class image of racing are responsible for the incredible paint jobs on today's rigs. The tractor and trailer are the biggest things that a sponsor can paint. As a result, some of the paint and decal jobs on the trailers rival any in existence.

The transporter usually leaves the factory with only the base coats of paint. When the design of the paint job has been decided upon, the large areas of color will be applied at a commercial paint shop. Choices of shops can be limited, as it takes a very large paint booth to accommodate a transporter. Once the base colors are on, the stickers that are used for most of the graphics and text in the design are applied. After the painting is finished, the team can begin to load the transporter.

When the trailer returns from the paint shop, it is time for the hard work to begin. The team members decide where everything is going to be located. They organize and label drawers and cabinets, set dividers, hooks, brackets, and shelves, and attend to many small details. Each team has individual preferences as to how it does things. I once sat and watched a truck driver mount cooling fans and ventilation ducts into the compartment where the team's radios were carried. He recounted a situation in which the radios did not function properly because they had overheated in transit. Now, whenever he is around a new trailer, this driver makes this particular modification. Often such information is fed back to the manufacturers and incorporated into future models.

If you read the list of the equipment needed at the track, then you can understand the need for the great deal of thought that is put into the design and layout of a Winston Cup transporter. The floors of the transporters are different from those of standard trailers. They are "dropped," meaning that the floor of the transporter is built much lower to the ground. This increases the cubic volume of available space by exploiting an area that is normally ignored in standard over-road trailers. More cubic

After being delivered to the team, the transporters and tractors are painted. The list of paint shops with a paint booth that can handle a job this big is limited. Only the base colors of the transporter are painted. The rest of the graphics and lettering will be applied with stickers.

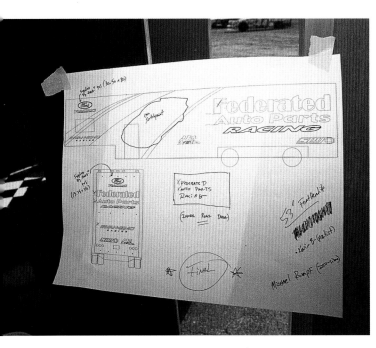

After the surface is thoroughly cleaned, the stickers are applied. Before the stickers are permanently mounted, they are first taped into place to assure that the layout is correct. Any mistake is both time consuming and expensive. The workers follow a blueprint, which supplies the proper locations for the stickers.

There is much work to be done before the truck will be ready to go to the track, as the teams make modifications to suit their particular needs. Here a team member is adding aluminum fixtures in the car-carrying area, so a little more gear can be fit into some unused space.

volume means more room for the team to carry more gear. By utilizing this space, designers maximize the carrying capacity while still staying within the dimensions allowed by law.

While this dropped floor design aids capacity, it does have some small drawbacks. By completely encasing the rear wheels, it is more difficult to cool them. This can mean tire or bearing problems due to heat building up. Teams often fabricate air ducts to feed cool air to these areas to help prevent overheating.

As the team members set out to load the transporter, they have a formidable job ahead. They must fig-

ure the most organized way to arrange the parts and tools that are to be carried to each event. However, storage capacity is not the only concern when dealing with transporters. Ergonomics and ease of use also must be factored into the equation. As a result, the layout of the transporter is of extreme importance, and from top to bottom it is a statement of form following function. Every space is taken advantage of, yet the equipment must be carried in a logical order so that the team members can find things quickly at the track. Items that will be needed the most often will be stored in the most accessible areas, while things that are rarely used will be

Small details can make a big difference. When the trucks park it is often dark, early in the morning or late at night. These powerful lights, mounted aft of the rear wheels, give the driver better vision when backing in tight quarters.

stored in less accessible areas. When storing parts, the team must figure out not only how to store everything, but also how to secure them so that they will not shift in the case of a rough ride on the way to a race. Not only is every square inch of the inside of the trailer utilized; the outside of the trailer also has compartments, wherever space is available. Many miscellaneous items can be stored here for easy access.

The typical Winston Cup transporter is divided into three main compartments: the lounge, located in the front of the trailer; the car area on top of the trailer; and the main compartment, which includes pretty much everything else. The car storage area is basically a shelf running from the back door of the transporter up to the lounge. Within it is room enough to secure two Winston Cup race cars (both the primary and backup) and a few miscellaneous parts. Recessed channels are built into the floor along the entire length of the car storage to provide

The sheer amount of equipment needed to successfully field a Winston Cup car is staggering. The hauler will be packed to the gills when it arrives in the garage area.

The car storage area before being loaded. The channels running the length of the floor have fixtures to attach tie-down straps to secure the car during transit.

It is a tight fit when the cars are rolled in. This is the backup car, loaded first. The primary car will be snugged up behind it. Note the fuel cans, for use during pit stops, stored over the car.

The top of the car carrier does more than keep the rain out of a Winston Cup transporter. The rear has been built tough to allow it to be used as a viewing platform. Collapsible handrails have been added for safety.

The lift folds up flat against the back of the transporter during transit. Like many other parts of the transporter, when it is not in use it is a billboard.

tie-down points, so that the cars can be strapped down to prevent them from rolling.

The cars are loaded using an electrically or hydraulically powered ramp on the back of the trailer. When the transporter is on the road, the ramp is folded flat against the back of the truck. When loading, the ramp is lowered, the car rolled on and raised to the level of the car storage compartment, and then rolled in and secured. The ramp is also used to load and unload heavy equipment into the main compartment of the transporter.

Even the top of the car storage area (the roof of the transporter) has more than one function. It must keep out the rain, but it also serves as a viewing platform for the team. As a result it has built-in safety rails to keep people from accidentally falling off. These rails are folded flat when the transporter is in transit. Team members can access the top of the transporter via two ladders that go from the ground to the lift and then from the lift to the top of the viewing area.

The main compartment is used for storage, a workspace, a kitchen, and a place to hide. When at the track,

Lifts may be electrically or hydraulically powered. Either way, they can lift over two tons without a problem.

the team members may use this area to meet and discuss strategy or to get out of the hustle and bustle of the garage area and eat a sandwich. This is especially nice during races in the summer months when the intelligence of the man who fitted an air conditioner to a transporter is most evident. The traditional layout for the main compartment has an aisle running down the center of the transporter with storage compartments and workspace located along each side. The floor of the aisle is padded with rubber mats to ease the stress of standing or walking on it all day. The aisle may be offset a bit to allow for deeper cabinets on one side. While all trailers differ somewhat, the typical layout has storage cabinets toward the front of the main compartment. A kitchen and workbench are usually located on the left side of the trailer, while more storage compartments fill the right side.

Storage comes in the form of cabinets, bins, and drawers. Each of these is usually labeled so that whatever is stored in it can be found quickly when it is needed. Cabinets house many medium and large sized cargoes. Some are set up with shelves and others with hooks. Whatever the case, all have methods to secure the cargo during transit. Truck drivers become very ingenious in keeping from having to reorganize items that shift or spill on the way to the track.

Bins are where large cargo, such as spare engines, are stored. These bins have removable doors to facilitate loading and unloading. The rest of the cargo is stored in the transporter's many drawers. Small parts and tools are organized and easy to find.

Regardless of type, the hardware in the storage compartments is first choice. Made of either polished stainless steel or chromed carbon steel, the storage compartments usually feature heavy-duty recessed hinges and latches. Not only is the interior of the transporter lined with bins and cabinets, every available space is used for storage and will include cabinets and bins accessible only from the outside of the transporter.

Even though it is the smallest part of the trailer and little physical work is done there, the lounge is a very

The lift is not only used to get the cars in and out of the transporter: It must also be used to get the toolbox and pit cart from the aisle, where they are strapped during transit.

The area outside of the back doors is a busy place during the race weekend. This "front porch" is used for everything from cooking lunch to getting an engine ready to drop into the car.

important place. More racing deals are discussed and made in the lounge of transporters than anywhere else. The lounge is shelter from the storm. Drivers and crews are great with fans and the press, but you have to keep in mind that the teams and drivers are working under a great deal of pressure. Failure at the track can mean job loss or physical harm to drivers and crew. This makes it difficult for all crew members, especially drivers and crew chiefs, to be amiable public figures all the time. And the better you are racing, the more intense it gets. When engaged in a championship battle toward the end of a season, the crew chief and driver will have to endure more and more interviews, and their garage stall and transporter will be crowded with fans and press. When a team has had its dreams and car destroyed by an accident or a mechanical failure, within minutes an interviewer will be grilling the driver or crew chief with some intelligent question such as, "How does it feel to have your car smashed to pieces and out of the race?" That is why you often see drivers and crew retreating to the transporter, where they can collect their thoughts and tempers before facing the racing public.

When traveling, the team's transporter is not only a place in which to haul the equipment and escape the pressures of the race. It also becomes the sponsor's flagship. When the 18 and 20 cars head out to the track, they represent Joe Gibbs Racing, but they also represent Interstate Batteries and Home Depot. Sponsors use the team as an advertising venue, and one of the perks of the sport is the opportunity to entertain. Whether it is large clients, valued vendors, or the company's own employees, a day at the track with the team is a wonderful experience for a company to give. It will turn the staunchest old boardroom grouch into a little boy again. The public relations manager for the team usually makes the arrangements,

providing passes and plenty of giveaways and privileges. The freebies might include shirts, hats, old tires, or in the event of a bad day, the mangled hood of a wrecked race car. One of the greatest privileges is going up to the top of the hauler to watch practice or going into the trailer's lounge to get out of the heat.

It would be interesting to see the CEO of a large company work with fans milling through his conference room during a board meeting, or the press shoving a microphone in his face seconds after he has learned that the stock price of his corporation just bottomed out. The importance of having somewhere to go and get away from it all cannot be overstressed. Drivers, owners, and crew usually do have RVs at most tracks where they can relax. However, while in the garage area the lounge in the trailer is the only true private refuge.

The view down the center aisle from front to back demonstrates the attention to utilizing every bit of usable space.

Left
The rear doors open into the center walkway, which runs the length of the transporter's main compartment and leads to the lounge.

An onboard climate control system keeps the transporter air conditioned in the summer and heated in the winter. Having a place to cool down or warm up can be a blessing in extreme weather.

Considering the limited space that transporter manufacturers have to work with, the interior of the main compartment is quite roomy, and quite a few people can move about inside.

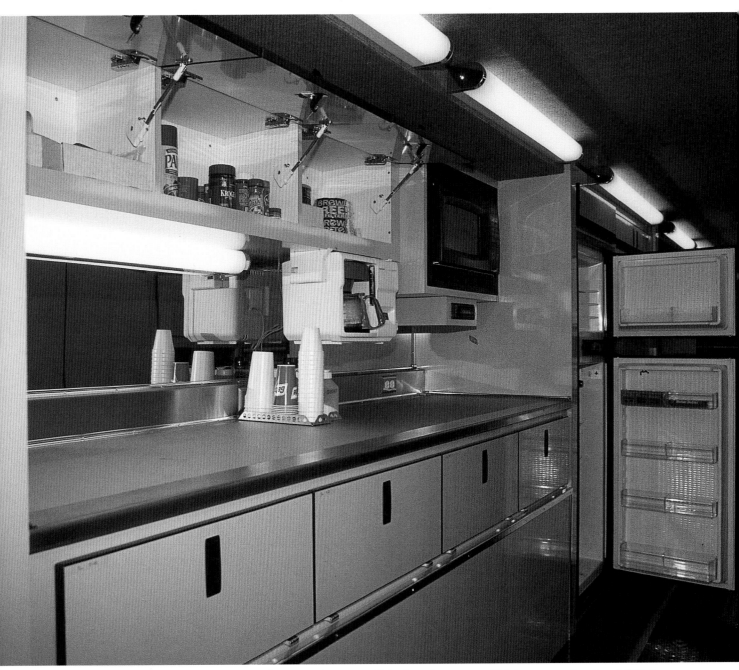

The galley features plenty of storage, a refrigerator, microwave, and lots of counter space on which to prepare a decent meal. With the usual addition of a gas grill outside, the team can have a steady diet of home-cooked food while on the road.

A small work area is incorporated into all transporters. It is a place to perform jobs requiring a clean space, or those requiring privacy. The transporter is one of the few places where a team can work with a complete sense of security. The workstation features drawers, a workbench, a vise, and electrical and compressed air supplies.

Computers have become essential tools for Winston Cup teams. While their use during the race and race practice is strictly limited, testing is another matter. Finding more speed is very difficult, and it greatly helps the team to know what the car is doing all the way around the track. Computers help the team understand the data gained through sensors and recording devices.

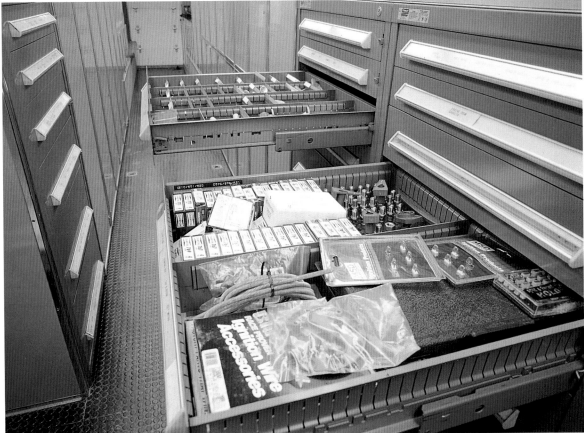

All drawers along the main compartment are labeled. Transporters carry too big a load for team members to remember exactly where everything is, and they must be able to find what they need quickly.

Cabinets come in all imaginable sizes, storing all types of gear. All of the parts and equipment must be well secured to prevent damage. Arriving with a broken part or tool is as bad as leaving it at home. If one thing breaks loose, it could damage other equipment as it bounces around.

Larger components, such as engines and generators, are housed in the bins, located on the same level as the walkway so items stored in them can easily be taken out. To further facilitate loading and unloading, the doors to the bins are removable.

Every available spot is taken advantage of. The areas along the sides and at the front of the transporter are no exception. These small storage areas will house a surprisingly large amount of gear.

The best place to relax in the garage area is the lounge. Different transporters offer different layouts and decoration. However, all have one thing in common—they are comfortable. Lounges give drivers, owners, and crew chiefs a quiet place to either get away from the crowds or, more often, to discuss racing matters. This may range from the best gear ratio for the race to who will be the team's next driver. At superspeedways, attempts to form drafting alliances may take place in the lounges before the race. It has been said that more racing deals are made in these lounges than anywhere else.

CHAPTER 4

DELIVERING THE LOAD

Did We Bring . . . ?

It is up to the team to properly load the transporter, and it is up to the truck driver to get it to the track. During the season it is the same routine week in and week out. After a Sunday race the truck driver leaves the track and heads to the shop. Obviously the location of the race dictates when the truck gets back to the shop. If the race is at Charlotte Motor Speedway, the trip may only be a few miles and the truck will be back to the shop Sunday evening. However, if the event is in Sonoma, California, the truck will have a trip of over 3,000 miles, and if the driver averages 65 miles per hour and only stops for an hour to get fuel, the earliest the transporter will be back at the shop is Tuesday night. During the week the team will unload and reload the transporter. Toward the end of the week—usually on Thursday—the transporter will head out to the next event.

Once the cars have been taken out of the transporter, the mass unloading begins. During this first assault there is little order as to what comes out. This is perhaps the best time to witness the diversity of the load. Coolers and clothes come out, as well as high-performance parts.

The loads carried by today's haulers are vast, and there are three issues that teams must address when loading the truck to go to a race: space, weight, and mix. Finding enough space for everything is the first problem. Many items that the teams must take to the track are large and bulky. Fitting all of it into the transporter is like working on a giant three-dimensional puzzle.

The second issue is staying under the Department of Transportation's legal weight limit for commercial trucks. In order to pass through the weigh stations on the highways and interstates, the truck's gross weight cannot exceed 80,000 pounds. The tractor usually weighs around 20,000 and the transporters usually weigh around 32,000 empty. Subtracting 7,200 pounds for two race cars (3,600 pounds each) leaves 20,800 pounds of spare parts and gear that can be taken to each race. Teams are often so close to this weight limit when the transporter leaves the shop that the truck driver can only fill the fuel tanks to half full. This means more stops for diesel fuel on the way to the track, but the team will be able to carry more gear.

The third factor in loading the transporter is making sure that the mix is right. The load that will be carried to a short track will be quite different from one carried to a superspeedway. Many of the parts used on the car are very different, including engines, transmissions, rear gears (for different ratios), brakes (heavier for short tracks), and coil springs. Some items, such as passenger windows and roof flaps, are used on a superspeedway but not on a short track, whereas heavy brake ducting will be used at short tracks but not on the longer ones.

NASCAR rigs do not run as many miles in a year as their true commercial counterparts. Trucking companies try to keep their rigs on the road as much of the time as possible. Tractors and transporters used by the Winston Cup teams travel only to races, practice sessions, and a few other special events. This usually accounts for 40 to 50 trips annually. With a team based in the Charlotte, North Carolina, area, the approximate round trip mileage for race travel alone is shown in the chart on the following page.

Getting ready to go to the track. The team piles the gear in a neat and orderly fashion for the truck driver to load.

Previous pages
The race really starts once the rig is pulled into place. Making sure everything is unloaded in the proper sequence and without any damage is a testament to the skills of the crew and transport driver.

What a mess! Every week each team sets up and tears down a workshop of equipment.

Track Location	Round trip mileage from Charlotte, NC		
Atlanta	1,120	Martinsville	480
Bristol	760	Michigan	2,680
California	4,840	North Carolina	360
Charlotte	80	Phoenix	4,280
Darlington	920	Pocono	2,440
Daytona	2,040	Richmond	1,120
Dover	1,960	Sears Point	5,560
Homestead	1,600	Texas	2,180
Indianapolis	1,240	Talladega	1,480
Las Vegas	4,480	Watkins Glen	1,360
Loudon	3,600	**Total for Year 2000**	**44,580**

Every bit of space counts. Even the lounge is used to carry some last-minute items. In here coolers, spare rims, and extra exhaust components fill the gaps.

While the Winston Cup life can be easier on a tractor than a life of hauling commercial loads, the schedule can be rough on the teams. Winston Cup team members spend a great deal of time away from home, and the truck drivers are no exception. Once at the track, they take on responsibilities like any other team member. With the use of private jets to wing the crew in and out of the track when needed, the truck driver often spends the most time on the road.

The tracks typically open for NASCAR Winston Cup teams on Friday morning at 6 A.M., and the teams expect the transporter to be sitting there when they arrive.

The truck driver must get up early, get ready, and have the truck at the gate of the speedway about 5:30 A.M.. Trucks drive through an access gate, over the track, and into the infield. Even at the tracks with tunnels, the trucks must cross the track because they are too big to go through the tunnels. Trucks are parked in the garage area based on the championship points standings. Watching the drivers park the transporters is an impressive demonstration of skill, especially at some of the short tracks. If you have ever been to Bristol, you must agree that it is a small miracle that so many trucks can be crammed into such a small place.

Fans in campers and the teams' transporters begin entering the track on a Friday morning at Talladega. After crossing the back straight, the campers head to the infield, as the transporters park in the garage area.

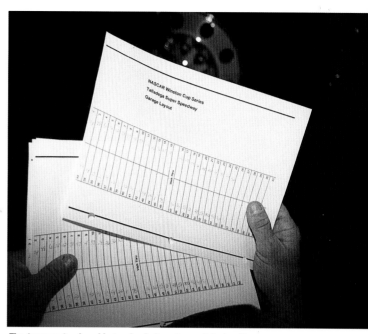

The transporters' parking order is based on point standings. NASCAR officials at the gate give each driver a map of the parking area as they enter.

As soon as the gate is opened on Friday morning the drivers head to the garage area. On the way in they receive their parking location from the NASCAR officials. Once the rigs are parked the unloading begins.

Before the center aisle of the transporter can be accessed, the tool box, pit cart, and crash cart must be unloaded. The pit and crash carts will not be used until race day and will be stored somewhere in the garage area. The tool box will be rolled to the garage stall to await the race car. These large rolling units, which are stored in the center aisle of the transporter during transit, are the team's primary mobile tool and parts sources and will be more thoroughly discussed the next chapter.

Following pages
The cars will be the first item unloaded. This enables crew members to get the car to the garage and begin to get it ready to hit the track.

Racks of rims are unloaded and taken to the Goodyear facility, which is located in the garage areas.

The primary race car is also quickly unloaded. The transporter's lift is lowered and the car comes off. Each team brings two cars to the track: the primary car and the backup car. Only the primary car is unloaded. The secondary car cannot be unloaded unless it is to be used in place of the primary. A team is not allowed to switch back and forth between cars. If the secondary car is brought out it is almost always because the primary car has been wrecked in qualifying or practice. However, occasionally a team's primary car handles so badly that they will try the backup to see if it is any more competitive. The race cars leave the shop with the team's best guess for the engine and handling package for the race. This allows the team to get the car on the track with a minimal amount of effort.

After the team members unload the car, they clear the center aisle of the transporter so they can get in. This space is usually occupied by the team's toolbox, pit cart, and crash cart.

Another of the first things to be done is the unloading of rims. Teams do not bring tires to the track; Goodyear brings the tires to the track. Teams bring their own rims and Goodyear sells and mounts the tires at its mounting and balancing facility at the track. Then the tires are brought back to the hauler and usually stacked outside the trailer. Teams may bring 8 to 10 sets of rims to a race.

Next to be unloaded from the transporter is the rather large amount of miscellaneous gear that the teams need for the race weekend. From gas cans to coolers, most of the transporter is so crammed full of stuff that for the trailer to be accessible, all of this gear must be cleared out and put somewhere. While some team members begin to get the race car ready, others continue to manage the load. As the interior of the transporter empties, the garage stall and area behind and to the sides of the transporter fill up. Only after all of this initial unloading can the team begin use the transporter as a work area.

During practice and qualifying, the monstrous load that the hauler carries pays off. Spare brakes are a must.

Pads will be changed on both front and rear brakes after practices. Calipers may also be swapped out before the race. Brakes are much more critical at short tracks and road courses where the drivers must rapidly decelerate upon entering the turns. On longer tracks there is much less demand on brakes. At Talladega and Daytona the drivers seldom use the brakes at all. Along with pads and calipers, the team brings spare master cylinders, brake lines, proportioning valves and fluid.

A wide variety of suspension parts are carried to the track. The setup of a race car is infinitely adjustable, and the suspension is the main thing that is changed when the team is searching for an optimal configuration. For a team to successfully adjust the car, there must be as many options as possible. Sway bars, which link the body and the suspension, will be brought in different thicknesses.

The thicker the bar, the less body roll the car will have. A thorough selection of springs is also a necessity, because each corner of the car will carry a different spring. A typical short-track setup may call for the following springs: right front, 1,200 pounds; left front, 1,100; right rear, 225; and left rear, 200. If this is the base setup, the team will likely carry extra springs both a bit stronger and a bit weaker for each corner of the car. Between races the load of springs will most likely be switched out. Spring rates change dramatically from track to track. Compare the short track setup above with a typical Talladega setup (right front, 3,200 pounds; left front, 2,000; right rear, 475; and left rear, 425). In addition to springs, the teams will bring spring rubbers—rubber inserts which, when placed between the coils of a spring, are a quick way to increase the spring pressure. The pit crew may put a rubber in during a pit stop or may start the race with a rubber and pull it out during a pit stop.

For many years the teams had to have many shock combinations for each track. A shock dyno could be found in each hauler. This device allows the teams to see exactly how the shock is performing before they mount it on the car. However, the rules were changed for the 2000 season. Teams will now be issued standard shocks for each race when they arrive at the track. These "tamperproof" shocks should have two results: The teams will spend less time and money on shocks, and the playing field should be leveled.

Other suspension components will also be brought to the track, including upper and lower control arms and trailing arms. In addition to serving as replacement parts in case of damage, many of these components have subtle differences that may change the geometry of the suspension. A very small variation in the suspension can mean a small but significant speed increase on the track. Small increases are what dialing in a setup is all about. The difference in being on the pole and not making the race last year at Martinsville in 2000 was 0.258 seconds.

While not usually considered setup items, many other suspension parts must come to the track. Ball joints, steering knuckles, idler arms, pitman arms, steering boxes, and columns are brought in case of failure. As well as stock parts, the crew must also have chassis and body materials in case of damage. If the primary car is slightly damaged during practice, the crew may elect to repair it instead of bringing out the backup car. This means that welders, torches, tubing, sheet metal, and fabrication tools must be brought. It is not uncommon for teams to fix bent tubing in the chassis and roll cage or to hang a new fender or quarter panel on the car. Extra front and rear fascia pieces, windshields, windows, hoods, deck lids, and spoilers must also be on hand. Alignment tools and scales on which to weigh the car are also frequently part of the trailer cargo.

When headed to a race, the typical NASCAR team hauler will have about 4,000 horsepower. This is due to the fact that each team brings around five engines to each race. Engine repairs are not common at the track, as engines are constantly tuned and checked. However, if a problem is seen, chances are the crew will immediately replace the engine. In the unlikely event that the team does run out of engines, it can bring another from the shop (difficult if you are racing in California and your shop is in Charlotte), or buy or rent an engine from another team.

Different teams have different philosophies concerning engines. Some have race engines and qualifying engines. Some talk about practice engines. Others seem to

be of the mind that if they build all of their engines the same, performance will always be consistent. Whatever the case, it usually takes a few engines to make it through the race weekend. Needless to say, if the engine blows it must be replaced. During practice an engine may log many laps, and it is wise to start the race with as fresh an engine as possible.

Teams will bring a large number of springs to the track. Changing the spring rate on each wheel is one of the fundamental ways to refine a setup.

A spare engine is not removed from the transporter until it is needed. Different transporters have different layouts, but more often than not the engines are carried in bins along the bottom of the inside of the hauler. The engines are mounted onto trolleys before being strapped into place in their compartments to keep them from being damaged during transit. When they are brought out at the track, they are unstrapped, rolled down the center aisle of the trailer, lowered using the ramp, and pushed to the garage. From there the team uses its engine hoist, brought to each race, to drop the engine into the car.

Other drive train components will also come to the track, including extra transmissions, drive shafts, and rear ends. The rear ends will be of different ratios so that the team can change gears when tuning the setup during practice.

Spare parts for the engine's auxiliary systems are also part of the hauler's cargo, so that ignition systems,

A team member gets a motor ready to go into the race car. Teams may arrive at the track with as many as five or six engines in the transporter.

Right
The great engine swap. After qualifying, all of the teams take out their "qualifying motor" and put in a practice motor.

distributors, and plug wires can be quickly swapped out if necessary. Spare carburetors, intake manifolds, and exhaust systems are available for quick changes. Spare power steering pumps and hardware, alternators, and starters are all stored for easy retrieval.

Other amenities will also be packed in the transporters. A gas grill, food, and beverages will help to keep the team fed over the weekend. Tarps and self-standing awnings will be brought to keep everything dry in case of rain.

It is a pressure-filled job being responsible for such a load week in and week out, especially when the cost of failure is so high. In jobs like this there is seldom any special recognition when the work is done right, but if something goes wrong the spotlight will be on.

Not all of the room is taken up with parts and tools. Supplies to keep the team fed and happy must be packed.

Opposite
Each week they set it up and tear it down. After the race on Sunday, the crews still have to load the truck back up and start the long road trip home. Here Bobby Labonte reviews the finishing results while the team loads the toolbox.

CHAPTER 5

WORKING AT THE TRACK

The Office on the Road . . .

Monday through Thursday, the teams have the luxury of working in some pretty nice shops. Many now feature every kind of automotive machining, fabrication, and testing equipment on the market. But on the weekends, when the effort shifts to the track, the environment is very close to what it was 40 years ago. The crowds are bigger and the equipment is nicer, but the team member working on the race car is still lying on the ground with a wrench in his hand. During the race weekend there are three primary areas in which the teams will work: in and around the transporter, in the track's garage area during qualifying and practice, and in the pit road during the race.

Once the transporter is parked on Friday morning, it will be the center of operations—meeting place, communications center, storage area, workshop, and sometimes just a place for a team member to escape to for a bite to eat and a cold drink. Nevertheless, before the transporter

The transporters are the center of activity leading up to the race. With the garage on one side and the transporters on the other, the middle ground can often be a hectic and crowded place to work.

can be used for any of these things, it must be unloaded. It is only after the bulk of the gear has been emptied from the transporter that it becomes a work area.

The small but very functional workbench placed along the side of the hauler is usually occupied. Here team members can take advantage of a relatively clean and private work area. A rubber-coated workbench, vise, and very good lighting all help the mechanic. Drawers under the workbench usually contain tools associated with the jobs done in this work area. Whether it is rebuilding a

While away from the shop, the transporter's work area still offers team members a place to work. Here a crew member rebuilds a shock after practice. The small workbench in the transporter gives the crew a small but clean environment to do delicate work on smaller parts.

shock or going through a carburetor, the mechanic will have everything that he needs close at hand.

While getting ready for the qualifying and the race, the team will primarily work on the car in the garage area. Most garages are designed so that when the rigs are parked, the back of the transporter will be pretty much directly across from the garage stall. This enables the crews to quickly access the parts and equipment that are stored in the transporter.

Once the team has been assigned a garage stall, members begin to set it up. The first thing that the teams put in this area is its large roll-around tool box, which contains all of the hand tools that the team will need. Jacks, jackstands, alignment equipment, and scales will also be in the garage area. The teams will have access to compressed air in the garage so they can take advantage of air tools.

The first activity on the track is qualifying practice, and as the action begins to heat up on the track it also heats up around the transporter and garage area. A qualifying setup need only be fast for one or two laps, while a race setup must be fast for longer runs, the length being determined by the distance that the car can go on a full tank of fuel. Because of this, qualifying can be the most hectic practice of the weekend. The routine is: Run a couple of laps, adjust the setup, then run a couple of more laps and adjust it again. Because the cars are only staying on the track for a couple of laps, there is a great deal of traffic in the garage. This means more traffic in the transporter and more race cars for the team members to dodge as they whip in and out of the garage area. In recent years, as the competition has become tighter and more teams are attempting to qualify, some teams will not make the race. The chance of not being fast enough to qualify for the race adds more pressure to this practice session.

Throughout qualifying practice, team members are always going in and out of the transporter, getting new springs, shocks, or any other part of the car that might need to be changed. There is also a steady stream of crew chiefs who spend practice running from the garage, where they can talk to their driver while the crew adjusts the race car, to the top of the hauler, where they can see the car run all of the way around the track.

In most qualifying formats, only the first 25 starting positions are determined on Friday. A second round will determine the rest of the starting positions on Saturday

After qualifying, Ricky Rudd heads to the top of the transporter to keep an eye on the competition. The viewing platform is an essential tool for the teams, allowing them to watch their own cars, and those of others, all the way around the track.

afternoon. As soon as Friday qualifying is over, teams will begin to change the setup on the car. If the team did not qualify, it can stand on its time and hope that it stands up, or attempt to requalify on Saturday. If the team chooses to requalify, it will leave the qualifying setup in the car and continue to refine it during the next practice session, when all of those who qualified are working on their race setups. This obviously puts a team at a disadvantage and underlines the necessity of making a solid qualifying effort.

Before the next practice session, the qualifying motor is taken out of the car and a fresh "practice motor" is put in. Suspension settings will be changed. A race setup must be fast over many laps, not just one or two. During race practice, a team may make short runs at first, and once members feel that they have a good setup, they can see how the car performs on long runs. The last practice before the race is "happy hour," a one-hour practice session after the Saturday race. A good setup during happy hour can mean sleeping peacefully the night before the race. If happy hour performance is less than satisfactory, the team may spend the night figuring out a new setup, and then go into the race not really knowing how the car will perform.

In the Pits

On Sunday morning the crew begins to set up the pit stall. A steady steam of crew members can be seen pushing equipment from the garage and transporters to pit road. The outline of the pit stall spaces is usually painted on the asphalt or concrete, marking the limits of each

As soon as the race car and the toolbox are taken from the transporter to the garage area, work begins. While some team members begin to get the car ready for the first practice, others continue to unload and organize the other gear.

team's usable space. The teams will arrange their gear around this perimeter, leaving as much room for crew members to move around as possible. A good bit of gear will fill the pit stall. The pit cart (discussed in the next section) is the centerpiece of the pit stall and usually the first piece of equipment to arrive at the site. Other gear includes a minimum of two lightweight aluminum jacks, four jack stands, a water tank, hammers and pry bars (to fix body damage), bins with parts and tools, and a boat-load of tires. Air guns, supplied with air from the air tanks in the pit cart, will be checked and air lines neatly coiled awaiting the first pit stop. Not only will essential racing gear be brought to the pits; a few creature comforts such

During practice the team will time the driver's lap speeds, and then it is back to the garage area. Drivers and crew chiefs then discuss how the car is handling and what adjustments can be made to make it faster.

On race day morning the teams begin to pull the equipment from the transporter and garage to the pit stall. It will take two or three hours to get the pit stall properly set up.

as umbrellas and coolers also will accompany the team. Banners will also make sure that the sponsors get their money's worth.

Carts and Boxes

Pit Cart

The centerpiece of the pit stall setup is the pit cart. These are hand-built by the teams with a great blend of functionality and showmanship. The pit cart houses many items that are likely to be used. Tools such as wrenches to adjust wedge or parts such as spring rubbers are placed where they can be easily retrieved. Today's pit carts will most likely house a television, VCRs, and a satellite dish. This allows the teams to watch the television broadcast as well as the live action on the track. If a team is running up front, it can be helpful for a crew chief to be able to watch his driver all the way around the track. Even if the team is not running up front, the broadcast

may still be helpful, as crew chiefs are able to watch the line the leader is taking around the track and see how it compares to their cars. The pit cart has a camera, which is extended out over the pit on a boom. This allows the team to film each pit stop so that performances can be evaluated and imperfections spotted. The pit cart also houses the air tanks, which supply the air for the airguns used during the pit stop.

The top of the pit box is usually converted to a viewing platform for crew chiefs, owners, and occasionally drivers' wives. The carts ride on large pneumatic tires so that they can traverse uneven ground with relative ease. A fold-up T-bar is used to push or pull the cart and to turn the front wheels.

Tool Carts

All the teams will bring a large roll-around tool box to the race. In it are kept all of the run-of-the-mill tools

The pit cart's satellite dish must be aligned if the team is going to have television access in the pits.

This pit stall is ready for the race to start, so some tires can be changed. Note the boom extending out and over the pit stall. On the end of the boom is a small camera, which is used to record the crew's pit stops.

needed to bring the car into competition. From wrenches to screwdrivers, any tool the team needs will be found in the roll-around. Also, keep in mind that each crew has to have more than one of each tool, because more than one team member may need a 5/8-inch wrench or a 3/8-inch-drive ratchet at one time.

Crash Carts

Teams must prepare for the worst and hope for the best. The crash cart is a piece of equipment in which the teams put a great deal of forethought, yet hope they will never have to use. But eventually, use them they will. The crash cart is the team's rescue squad. Stored on and

in it are parts that are commonly damaged in what could be called "light crashes." Often, if a team is caught up in a wreck, the damage is sufficient to force the car off the track but not out of the race. For instance, if the team suffers damage to the left front of the car, there may be damage to the oil cooler, which is mounted behind the grill. This may only be a five-minute repair, and if the team can change it during a yellow flag, they may not go many laps down. As a result, an extra oil cooler and all of the mounting hardware are carried on the crash cart, along with other items such as suspension components. Unlike the pit

continued on page 94

You have to have it, but you hope to never use it. The crash cart is only used in worst case scenarios, when the car has been damaged and must be repaired before going back on the track.

Teams try to load the crash cart with everything that could possibly be damaged and quickly repaired. Many of the parts on the crash cart are suspension components, which in the case of damage will be used to get the car running true. From control arms and trailing arms to entire rear axles, the parts and mounting hardware are easily accessible.

Most of the waiting is done on the inside of the wall, but the work is done on the outside. Pit crew members all have other duties before the race, but the two minutes (seven pit stops at 18 seconds each) they work over the wall is the most critical.

The capacity of these carts is staggering. They hold more than just tools and parts. Gear ranging from televisions to thermometers helps the crew and crew chief have a more complete understanding of their environment.

Opposite
A crew chief's office during the race. Data are valuable to Winston Cup teams. Even information gained in a losing effort may be very valuable when the team returns for the next race at a track.

Some serious toolboxes are taken to the track. The toolbox, usually the first item taken to the garage, provides the teams with the more common hand tools used to work on the cars.

Right
The toolbox will have to have more than one of most items. At any given time, there is no telling how many of the crew will need a 9/16-inch wrench.

cart and the tool carts, the crash cart has no sides, doors, or drawers. As repairs will always be made under high-pressure situations, the teams don't want to lose a second looking for something.

Conclusion

As teams head into the twenty-first century, it is a sure bet that advancements in the transporters will continue. The physical size of the transporters is already at the maximum allowed by law, so the area most likely to be affected will be in weight reduction. Because the gross weight of the tractor, trailer, and load cannot exceed 80,000 pounds, any weight removed from the tractor or transporter can be used for additional cargo.

Trailer manufacturers now offer some options in this area, but they do so at a substantial cost. Weight savings are often accomplished by using materials that are both strong and lightweight, such as aluminum, titanium, and carbon fiber. But these special materials are expensive, so the result is the lighter the transporter gets, the more it costs the team. But if a team can get an edge at the track with another ton of gear, the additional cost is worth it. The difference in the additional purchase cost can be made recovered just by finishing a few positions higher in one or two races.

Either way, reduced rig weight, or increased load allowance it will not solve the truck driver's problem. As one Winston Cup truck driver put it, "If they got the total weight of the tractor and trailer down to ten pounds, it would allow the team to carry 79,990 pounds of gear. But I guarantee I would still get tickets for being over the weight limits on the way to the race. They just won't quit piling things on the trailer!"

The pit cart is the centerpiece of the pit stall. Many are custom built by the teams to fit their particular needs.

Opposite
The pit area is not used during practice and qualifying, but it makes up for it on race day. As the week progresses, the teams work in a smaller and smaller area. From the roomy shop they go to the congested garage area and then to pit area, which often resembles a trading pit on Wall Street.